MY FIRST TURKEY

ALL ABOUT TURKEY FOR KIDS

Copyright 2023 by Globed Children Books

All rights reserved. No part of this book may be reproduced or distributed in any form without prior written permission from the author, with the exception of non-commercial uses permitted by copyright law.

Limited of Liability/Disclaimer of Warranty: The publisher and author make no representations or liabilities with respect to the accuracy and completeness of the contents of this work and specifically disclaim all warranties including without limitations warranties of fitness of particular purpose. No warranty may be created or extended by sales or promotional materials. This work is sold with the understanding that the publisher and author is not engaging in rendering medical, legal or any other professional advice or service. Further, readers should be aware that websites listed in this work may have changed or disappeared between when this work was written and when it is read.

Interior and cover Design: Daniel Day
Editor: Margaret Bam

For My Sons, Daniel, David and Jude

The Blue Mosque in Istanbul

Turkey

Turkey is a **country**.

A country is land that is controlled by a **single government**. Countries are also called **nations, states, or nation-states**.

Countries can be **different sizes**. Some countries are big and others are small.

Istanbul Cityscape

Where Is Turkey?

Turkey is located in the continent of **Asia**.

A continent is **a massive area of land that is separated from others by water or other natural features**.

Turkey is situated in **Western** Asia.

Ankara Aerial view

Capital

The capital of Turkey is Ankara.

Ankara is located in the **north-western part** of the country.

Istanbul is the largest city in Turkey.

The Ortakoy Mosque in Istanbul

Regions

Turkey is a country that is made up of seven regions.

The regions of Turkey are as follows:

Marmara region, Aegean region, Mediterranean Region, Central Anatolian, Eastern Anatolian, Southern Anatolian Region and Black sea region.

Turkish man and Turkish flag

Population

Turkey has population of around **86 million people** making it the 17th most populated country in the world and the 9th most populated country in Asia.

The Galata Tower in Turkey

Size

Turkey is **783,562 square kilometres** making it the 10th largest country in Asia by area.

Turkey is the 37th largest country in the world.

Languages

The official language of Turkey is Turkish. Turkish is the most widely spoken of the Turkic languages, with around 80 to 90 million speakers.

Here are a few Turkish phrases
- **Selam! - Hello**
- **Teşekkürler - Thank you**
- **Adınız nedir? - What's your name?**
- **Güle güle! - Bye bye!**
- **Kaç yaşındasınız? - How old are you?**

Pamukkale

Attractions

There are lots of interesting places to see in Turkey.

Some beautiful places to visit in Turkey are

- **Hagia Sophia (Aya Sofya) Mosque**
- **Ephesus**
- **Cappadocia**
- **Topkapı Palace**
- **Pamukkale**

The Maiden's Tower in Turkey

History of Turkey

People have lived in Turkey for a very long time. In fact, Turkey is one of the world's earliest permanently settled regions.

Modern Turkey was inhabited by many ancient civilisations including the Hattians, Hittites, Anatolian peoples, Mycenaean Greeks, Persians and others.

The Turkish War of Independence resulted in the abolition of the Sultanate, the signing of the Treaty of Lausanne and the proclamation of the Republic.

The Blue Mosque, Turkey

Customs in Turkey

Turkey has many fascinating customs and traditions.

- Coffee is a very popular drink in Turkey. Many Turkish people drink coffee every day and believe that it can be used to predict the future.
- Many Turkish people celebrate Hıdırellez. This festival symbolizes the beginning of the spring and waking up in nature and celebrates the night the Prophets Hıdır and İlyas met.

Turkish folk dance team

Music of Turkey

There are many different music genres in Turkey such as **Turkish music, Turkish folk music, traditional folk music, Ottoman music and Turkish pop music.**

Some notable Turkish musicians include
- **Ajda Pekkan**
- **Hadise**
- **Şebnem Ferah**
- **Zülfü Livaneli**
- **Derya Uluğ**

Manti

Food of Turkey

Turkey is known for having delicious, flavoursome and rich dishes.

The national dish of Turkey is **Manty or Manti** which is delicious Turkish dumplings with spiced ground meat, served with garlic yoghurt and spices infused olive oil.

Doner Kebap

Food of Turkey

Some popular dishes in Turkey include

- **Piyaz**
- **Ezogelin corba**
- **Saksuka**
- **Kisir**
- **Mercimek kofte**
- **Yaprak dolma**
- **Inegol kofte**
- **Iskender kebab**

The Bosphorus Bridge in Istanbul

Weather in Turkey

Turkey has a **Mediterranean climate** with hot dry summers and mild winters.

The hottest month of the year is July and the coldest month is January.

Horses in Turkey

Animals of Turkey

There are many wonderful animals in Turkey.

Here are some animals that live in Turkey

- **Caracal**
- **Gray wolf**
- **Dolphins**
- **Fallow deer**
- **Eurasian lynx**
- **Black vulture**
- **Northern bald Ibis**
- **Chevrotain**

Beaches

There are many beautiful beaches in Turkey which is one of the reasons why so many people visit this beautiful country every year.

Here are some of Turkey's beaches

- **Kleopatra Beach**
- **Gocek Beach**
- **Icmeler Beach**
- **Kaputas beach**
- **Kabak Beach**

Playing football

Sports of Turkey

Sports play an integral part in Turkish culture. The most popular sport is **Soccer.**

Here are some of famous sportspeople from Turkey

- **Olcay Şahan - Footballer**
- **Mustafa Dağıstanlı - Wrestling**
- **Elvan Abeylegesse - Athletics**
- **Mesut Bakkal - Footballer**

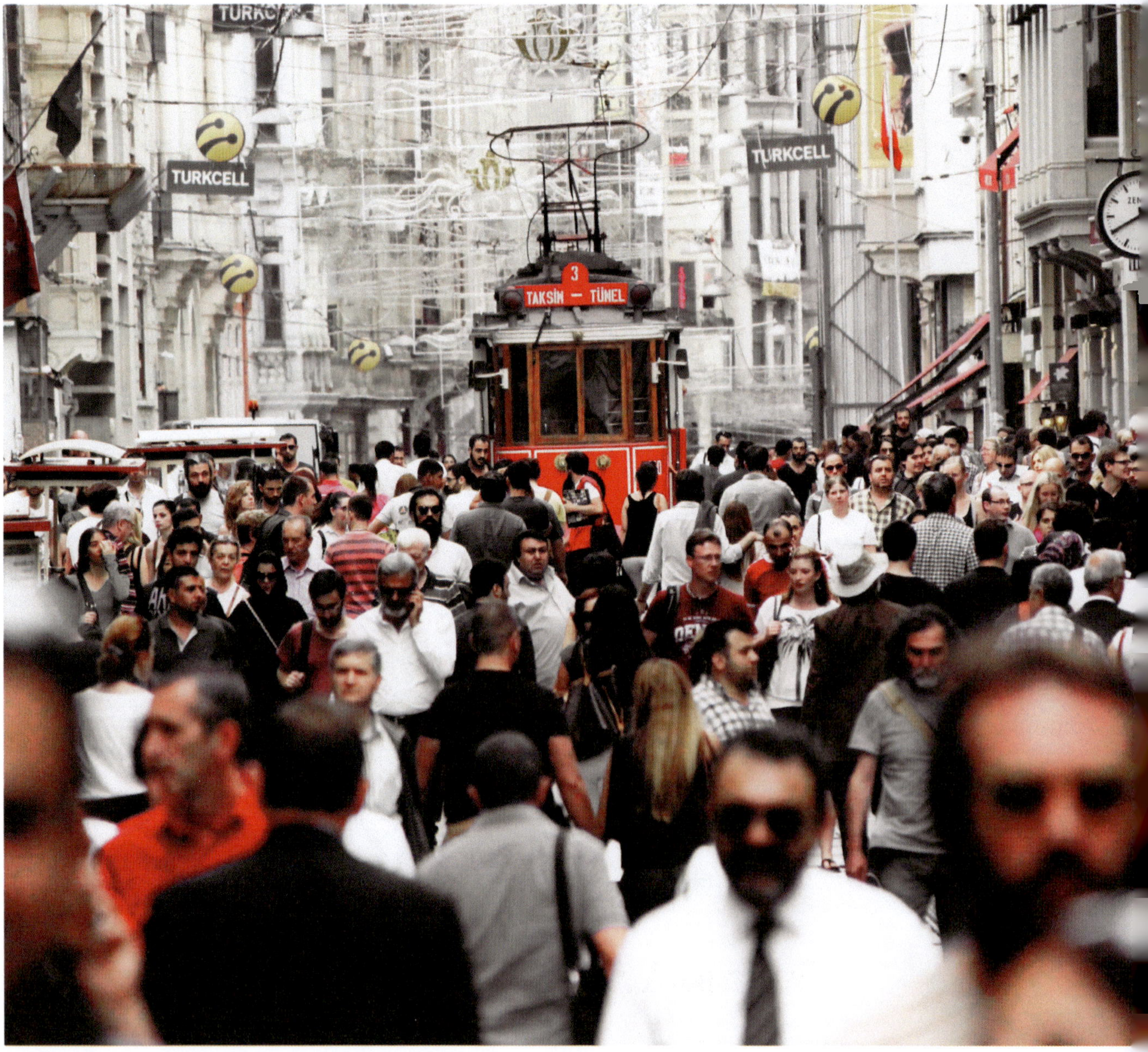
TURKCELL
TURKCELL
3
TAKSIM — TÜNEL

Famous

Many successful people hail from Turkey.

Here are some notable Turkish figures

- **Orhan Pamuk - Novelist**
- **Tarkan - Singer**
- **Ahmet Ertegun - Songwriter**
- **Mehmed II - Ruler**
- **Arda Turan - Footballer**

Grand Bazaar, Istanbul

Something Extra...

As a little something extra, we are going to share some lesser known facts about Turkey.

- **Turkey is home to one of the world's biggest and oldest malls.**
- **Santa Claus actually comes from Turkey.**

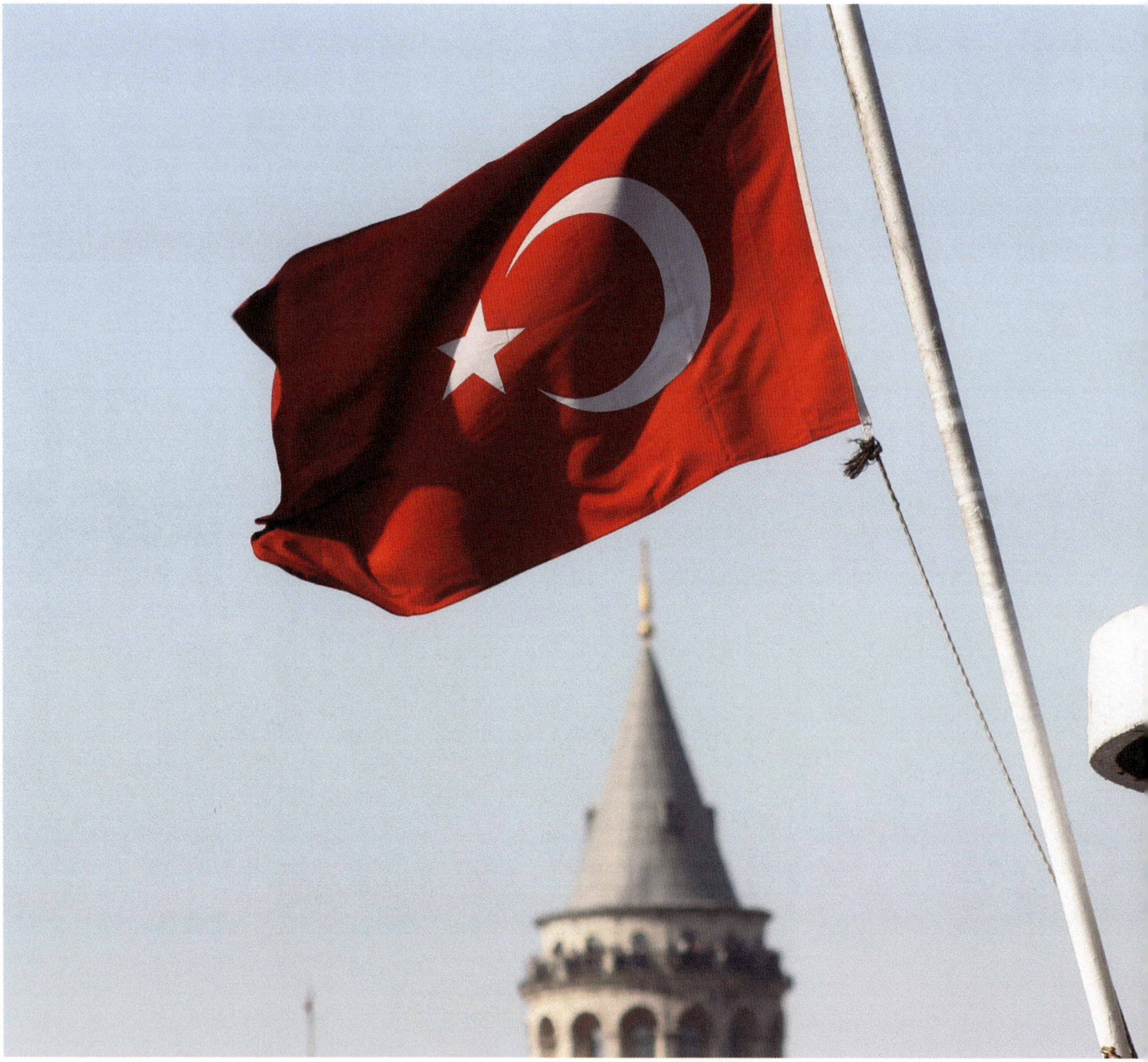

Words From the Author

We hope that you enjoyed learning about the wonderful country of Turkey.

Turkey is a country rich in culture and beauty, with lots of wonderful places to visit and people to meet.

We hope you continue to learn more about this wonderful nation. If you enjoyed this book, consider leaving a review!

With Love

Printed in Great Britain
by Amazon